THE
SMART
HANDBOOK

Science-Based Tools
To Get **it Done

ELIZABETH YIANNOULIS

AKNOWLEDGEMENT

Thank you, Dr. Andrew Huberman.
Thank you, Pat, for your SMART skills.
Thank you to my consigliere, Francesco.
Lastly, to all those who have supported me,
and continue to support me,
thank you for believing.

Dedicated to my beautiful childre

THE S.M.A.R.T. APPROACH

What is stopping you from achieving your goals? Is it sleeping in, staying up too late, scrolling on social media, drinking a little too much wine at that business dinner, work/life balance, procrastinating, family obligations? Kids…oh, the kids.

We all have great excuses as to why we haven't accomplished our goals, but what if I tell you that you CAN accomplish your goal in 90 days. You just need to start with the right approach, backed by science. Start by doing one thing: write down your S.M.A.R.T. goals: specific, measurable, attainable, realistic, and timely.

S.M.A.R.T. was developed by George Doran, Arthur Miller, and James Cunningham in their 1981 article "There's a S.M.A.R.T. way to write management goals and objectives" [i] and it works. Just Google *data from peer-reviewed studies with S.M.A.R.T. goals*. The results will speak for themselves.

Many people struggle to accurately write down their S.M.A.R.T. goals. This handbook will provide examples of what to do and what not to do when writing your S.M.A.R.T. goals.

Now let's take a closer look at understand S.M.A.R.T.

THE ACRONYM
S.M.A.R.T.

SPECIFIC

Pick one specific goal you would like to achieve. Include the verb/action you must complete to pursue your goal, a unit of measurement, and, if applicable, which days and time of day you will pursue your goal. "Getting in shape," for example, is not a specific goal. Let's break it down.

The specific goal	To lose body fat.
Measurable	5 pounds.
The verb/action	Resistance training.
Day/Time/Duration	Every Tuesday, Thursday and Saturday before work between 6:30–8am for a duration of 40 minutes.
Summary	To lose 5 pounds of body fat by resistant training every Tuesday, Thursday and Saturday before work between 6:30-8am for a duration of 40 minutes.

MEASURABLE

Monitoring your progress using a unit of measure is key to succeeding in achieving your goal. A unit of measurement could be time/duration, number of repetitions, or pounds/kilograms just to mention a few. Each time you complete the verb/action, document the unit of measurement appropriate for your specific goal, such as using a spreadsheet, an app, or calendar. There is no right or wrong way to document your progress. Understand what method works best for you to stay consistent.

ATTAINABLE

The right tools and resources can also assist you in attaining your goal. Ask yourself: "Do I have access to the tools and resources required to successfully achieve my goal?"

REALISTIC

Is your goal aligned with your values? And what will get in the way of you achieving it? These questions will guide you in understanding whether your goal is realistic. For example, family value may limit your availability at certain times of the day.

TIMELY

The science literature supports a 90-day time frame to achieve a goal. Why 90 days? If you set a goal for 30 days, it may be not challenging enough to activate the arousal network. If you set a goal for one-year, you may become disengaged in the middle of pursuing your goal and lose the motivation to achieve your goal.

MOTIVATION AND GOAL-SETTING TOOLS

The two approaches we can use when setting goals are APPROACH goals or AVOIDANCE goals. An approach goal is, for example, wanting to complete 10 push-ups in a row with proper form. An example of an avoidance goal is to avoid eating unhealthy foods. Set an approach goal for greater success.

Make your goal measurable: a number.

Set your own goals. You hold yourself more accountable when you set your own goals. So, don't ask a coach to set the goal for you.

Be in the same psychological state when setting the goal. If your goals verb/action is to work out at 5 a.m. three days a week, be at the gym working out at 5 a.m. when you set that goal, not while you are sitting by the pool on a Friday afternoon.

Create a buffer of three-to-five days a month for emergency purposes. Being kind and realistic to yourself goes a long way and keeps you motivated.

If you reward yourself at every milestone, you are reducing motivation overall. An intermittent reward system—literally tossing a coin—will avoid that. So, if you lost 2 pounds and want to reward yourself with a cheesecake, toss a coin. Heads you eat the cheesecake, tails you eat the cheesecake at another milestone.

Set a lofty goal. A goal just out of reach stimulates your arousal network to get you into action.

Science tells us that being in a safe, but uncomfortable state allows us to make change and progress. Step out of your comfort zone.

Pair a task you don't have the motivation to complete with something you enjoy doing. The caveat: only link the enjoyable task to the one task you find to be unmotivating.

Use visual focus to increase/maintain motivation. Cognitive focus, readiness and mental state are linked to your visual system (the eyes are part of the brain). When you become distracted, visually focus on something that is the same distance of the task you were distracted from and stare at that object for 30–90 seconds. For example, if you are completing research on your laptop and become unfocused, focus on an object that is the same distance from your laptop, for example, your mouth, a pen, a dot on a piece of paper. Hold your gaze for 30–90 seconds on the one object and then continue with your task of research.

We are excited to kick-start our goal. And when the finish line is near, we once again are ecstatic. The middle, however, if too long, can cause you to become discouraged, distracted or to lose motivation. To avoid a lengthy middle, make your goal short term. The science supports 90–days. It might also be helpful to include milestones.

RECOMMENDATIONS

Quality sleep helps with recovery, mental health, and learning. Are you getting eight hours of sleep? The Huberman Lab *Toolkit for Sleep* is a great resource which discusses sleep protocols.[i]

Hydrate throughout the day. It's great for your skin, recovery, cognition, focus, and so much more.

Try to get natural sunlight in the morning and just before sunset for five-to-15 minutes. Try your best to sleep in a dark room.

The food choices you make affect your energy level.

Strength training is a great way to keep your mind sharp.

There can be more than one potential verb/action to achieve your goal. You decide what works best for you.

Limit the amount of time you spend watching the news and scrolling aimlessly on social media.

Happy hormones include: endorphins with exercise (especially running); dopamine by listening to music; serotonin with getting out into the sun; and, oxytocin with physical contact.

Include the term "non-negotiable" in your vocabulary.

Continuously ask yourself "Is what I am doing right now adding value to my end goal?"

Doing something "just in case" is a waste of time.

Understand your strengths at various times of the day. For example, perhaps your best time for focus is before lunch. Plan accordingly.

Profit/monetary gains is a result of your goal.

Procrastination is essentially avoiding an emotional state. Ask yourself what feeling are you avoiding.

You must think things through carefully—but don't over-think. At some point you must stop doing research and just go. What are you afraid of? Failure? Just do and you won't fail.

Don't be fooled: you are not missing out on anything by not attending that party tonight.

Who controls who? Does your phone control you, or do you control your phone?

Don't let all the noise around you distract you. Be *present* and in the moment (even if you think daydreaming will make you feel better).

Social media has given everyone a microphone. Whose microphone are you listening to?

Meditation can help with focus.

Growth mindset is key. As Master Oogway said in *Kung Fu Panda*, "You must believe."

The following pages demonstrate some examples of S.M.A.R.T. goals. You decide on the ones that are actionable versus those that are missing pieces of information.

SUB-OPTIMAL S.M.A.R.T. FITNESS GOAL

SPECIFIC
Get in better shape by working out.

MEASURABLE
Weigh myself every day.

ATTAINABLE
It is attainable because I have a gym membership.

REALISTIC
It is realistic because I am motivated to get into better shape.

TIMELY
To get in better shape in 1-2 months.

OPTIMAL S.M.A.R.T. FITNESS GOAL

SPECIFIC

I will lose 8 pounds of body fat by completing 40 minutes of resistance training three times a week before work on Monday, Wednesday, and Friday.

MEASURABLE

I will weigh myself every morning between 6am–7am using a Withings scale to measure body weight and composition and record the results in my calendar.

ATTAINABLE

I have the resource I need including fitness equipment and a Withings scale. I have the knowledge of health and fitness to help with my journey.

REALISTIC

This is realistic because I have the motivation to get into better shape for my long-term health. I want to be able to move with my children. The things that can get in the way of completing my morning workout are my children, however that distraction can be mitigated by working out before they wake up. If I miss one day during the week, I will work out Saturday morning before the kids wake up.

TIMELY

My goal is to lose the 8 pounds in 90 days.

S.M.A.R.T. HEALTH AVOIDANCE GOAL

SPECIFIC

I will avoid sugar-drinks (soda, juice, alcohol).

MEASURABLE

I will ensure there is a tally of zero each day of sugar drinks.

ATTAINABLE

I will avoid sugared drinks.

REALISTIC

I have gone without sugared drinks before. When I am in a social environment, I will avoid them by drinking water with lemon.

TIMELY

For the next 30 days.

S.M.A.R.T. HEALTH APPROACHABLE GOAL

SPECIFIC

I will drink 2.5 liters of water a day – 1 liter before lunch, 1 liter before dinner and .5 liter with dinner.

MEASURABLE

I will place five elastic bands over my 500ml reusable water bottle and remove an elastic band each time I finish the bottle. Keep a spreadsheet with number of elastic bands remaining to see how short I was from my goal of 2.5 liters of water each day.

ATTAINABLE

I have access to water, a reusable water bottle and elastic bands. I have all the tools and resources I need to complete my goal.

REALISTIC

It aligns with my values of wanting to improve the health of me and my family. I will be prepared mentally when in environments where other drinking options are available. For example, when at a business dinner, I will drink water in lieu of wine.

TIMELY

After 90 days for this to be a new habit.

SUB-OPTIMAL S.M.A.R.T.
NEW SKILL GOAL

SPECIFIC

Be able to communicate in French.

MEASURABLE

Using the App to monitor my progress.

ATTAINABLE

I have an app I can use.

REALISTIC

Yes, the goal is realistic because I already know the basics.

TIMELY

To accomplish my goal in 30 days.

OPTIMAL S.M.A.R.T. NEW SKILL GOAL

SPECIFIC

To have a five-minute conversation with a French speaker by practicing French 20 minutes every morning before work through conversation, (question and answers) using full sentences.

MEASURABLE

I will time myself with question and answers every Saturday, aiming to improve by 20 seconds each week.

ATTAINABLE

I have the time in the morning and the app to assist in full sentences. I also have access to a French radio and French movies.

REALISTIC

Speaking French has been a passion of mine since I was a child and am highly motivated to be able to have a conversation in French. The only thing that would get in the way is if something of importance takes my time in the morning before work. I can mitigate that putting time aside during my lunch to practice.

TIMELY

To accomplish this goal in 90 days and then set a new goal after that.

S.M.A.R.T. NEW HABIT AVOIDANCE GOAL

SPECIFIC

Avoid being on my cell phone after 9pm.

MEASURABLE

Put an X on my calendar at 9pm to acknowledge I put my phone away at 9pm that night.

ATTAINABLE

I will set my alarm on my phone at 8:59pm and turn my phone on *DO NOT DISTURB*.

REALISTIC

Yes, the goal is realistic. I like to think I control my phone and that my phone doesn't control me.

TIMELY

Two weeks.

S.M.A.R.T. NEW HABIT APPROACHABLE GOAL

SPECIFIC

Using my cell phone for social media 20 minutes a day with 10 minutes allocated in the morning and 10 minutes allocated in the evening by logging off after each use.

MEASURABLE

Monitor my screentime with the data on my smartphone app.

ATTAINABLE

I have created this habit of when bored to just go to my phone for a short fix, but I acknowledge that and will correct it by refocusing when I am bored on being present in the moment.

REALISTIC

I have the motivation to spend less time scrolling on social media because I would like to spend more time focusing my family and friends, and to be present. Yes, I can be tempted to scroll social media, as it has become a habit, but with a barrier of having to log into my account, I will take that moment to reflect on the choices I am making in the moment.

TIMELY

Knowing this is a new habit I am creating; I would like to focus on this new habit for 30 days and then re-evaluate.

S.M.A.R.T. MONETARY BUSINESS GOAL

SPECIFIC

To earn $250,000 in commission.

MEASURABLE

I will work backward from $250,000 and every time I make a sale, minus the commission from my goal.

ATTAINABLE

It is attainable because last year I earned $200,000 and just need to make an additional $50,000.

REALISTIC

Yes, it is realistic because I have the knowledge and motivation needed to commit to this goal.

TIMELY

To accomplish this goal by the end of the year.

OPTIMAL S.M.A.R.T. BUSINESS GOAL

SPECIFIC

Close three deals prospecting expired listings every Monday, Tuesday and Thursday from 9am–12:00pm: sending out expired letters, and door knocking every Wednesday from 5pm–7pm in the area of expired listings I am focusing.

MEASURABLE

Make a total of 25 contacts a week (5 per weekday). A contact being when they have answered the question if they are planning on making a move in the next 3–6 months. To be entered into accountability app daily.

ATTAINABLE

I have the resources needed from our team folder including expired letters and knowledge in finding expired listings.

REALISTIC

It can be challenging to work with clients who have been disappointed in the past with agents, but I enjoy that challenge of changing the client's mindset and providing confidence to my clients as that is aligned with my core values.

TIMELY

Measure every three months and to be reviewed with my team lead.

YOUR S.M.A.R.T. GOAL
FOR THE NEXT 90 DAYS

SPECIFIC

MEASURABLE

ATTAINABLE

____

____

____

____

REALISTIC

____

____

____

____

TIMELY

____

____

____

____

HOW TO DOCUMENT
THE NEXT 90 DAYS

Each day, commit to your one non-negotiable task for the day to get you one step closer to your end goal. It could be five minutes; it could be 20 minutes. Just commit. Remember, taking a day off can be beneficial for your end goal. Let's have fun and enjoy the process.

Day 1 ____

Today's non-negotiable to accomplish my goal:

Day 2 ____

Today's non-negotiable to accomplish my goal:

Day 3 ____

Today's non-negotiable to accomplish my goal:

Day 4 ____

Today's non-negotiable to accomplish my goal:

Day 5 ____

Today's non-negotiable to accomplish my goal:

Day 6 ____

Today's non-negotiable to accomplish my goal:

Day 7 ____

Today's non-negotiable to accomplish my goal:

Day 8 ____

Today's non-negotiable to accomplish my goal:

Day 9

Today's non-negotiable to accomplish my goal:

Day 10

Today's non-negotiable to accomplish my goal:

Day 11____

Today's non-negotiable to accomplish my goal:

Day 12____

Today's non-negotiable to accomplish my goal:

Day 13

Today's non-negotiable to accomplish my goal:

Day 14

Today's non-negotiable to accomplish my goal:

Day 15____

Today's non-negotiable to accomplish my goal:

Day 16____

Today's non-negotiable to accomplish my goal:

Day 17____

Today's non-negotiable to accomplish my goal:

Day 18____

Today's non-negotiable to accomplish my goal:

Day 19____

Today's non-negotiable to accomplish my goal:

Day 20____

Today's non-negotiable to accomplish my goal:

Day 21

Today's non-negotiable to accomplish my goal:

Day 22

Today's non-negotiable to accomplish my goal:

Day 23____

Today's non-negotiable to accomplish my goal:

Day 24____

Today's non-negotiable to accomplish my goal:

Day 25

Today's non-negotiable to accomplish my goal:

Day 26

Today's non-negotiable to accomplish my goal:

Day 27______________________________________

Today's non-negotiable to accomplish my goal:

Day 28______________________________________

Today's non-negotiable to accomplish my goal:

Day 29

Today's non-negotiable to accomplish my goal:

Day 30

Today's non-negotiable to accomplish my goal:

Day 31______________________________________

Today's non-negotiable to accomplish my goal:

Day 32______________________________________

Today's non-negotiable to accomplish my goal:

Day 33

Today's non-negotiable to accomplish my goal:

Day 34

Today's non-negotiable to accomplish my goal:

Day 35

Today's non-negotiable to accomplish my goal:

Day 36

Today's non-negotiable to accomplish my goal:

Day 37

Today's non-negotiable to accomplish my goal:

Day 38

Today's non-negotiable to accomplish my goal:

Day 39____

Today's non-negotiable to accomplish my goal:

Day 40____

Today's non-negotiable to accomplish my goal:

Day 41

Today's non-negotiable to accomplish my goal:

Day 42

Today's non-negotiable to accomplish my goal:

Day 43____

Today's non-negotiable to accomplish my goal:

Day 44____

Today's non-negotiable to accomplish my goal:

Day 45____

Today's non-negotiable to accomplish my goal:

Day 46____

Today's non-negotiable to accomplish my goal:

Day 47____

Today's non-negotiable to accomplish my goal:

Day 48____

Today's non-negotiable to accomplish my goal:

Day 49_______________________________

Today's non-negotiable to accomplish my goal:

Day 50_______________________________

Today's non-negotiable to accomplish my goal:

Day 51

Today's non-negotiable to accomplish my goal:

Day 52

Today's non-negotiable to accomplish my goal:

Day 53______________________________________

Today's non-negotiable to accomplish my goal:

____

____

____

____

____

____

Day 54______________________________________

Today's non-negotiable to accomplish my goal:

____

____

____

____

____

Day 55____

Today's non-negotiable to accomplish my goal:

Day 56____

Today's non-negotiable to accomplish my goal:

Day 57____

Today's non-negotiable to accomplish my goal:

Day 58____

Today's non-negotiable to accomplish my goal:

Day 59____

Today's non-negotiable to accomplish my goal:

Day 60____

Today's non-negotiable to accomplish my goal:

Day 61

Today's non-negotiable to accomplish my goal:

Day 62

Today's non-negotiable to accomplish my goal:

Day 63____

Today's non-negotiable to accomplish my goal:

Day 64____

Today's non-negotiable to accomplish my goal:

Day 65

Today's non-negotiable to accomplish my goal:

Day 66

Today's non-negotiable to accomplish my goal:

Day 67____

Today's non-negotiable to accomplish my goal:

____

____

____

____

____

____

____

Day 68____

Today's non-negotiable to accomplish my goal:

____

____

____

____

____

____

Day 69____

Today's non-negotiable to accomplish my goal:

Day 70____

Today's non-negotiable to accomplish my goal:

Day 71____

Today's non-negotiable to accomplish my goal:

Day 72____

Today's non-negotiable to accomplish my goal:

Day 73

Today's non-negotiable to accomplish my goal:

Day 74

Today's non-negotiable to accomplish my goal:

Day 75____

Today's non-negotiable to accomplish my goal:

Day 76____

Today's non-negotiable to accomplish my goal:

Day 77____

Today's non-negotiable to accomplish my goal:

Day 78____

Today's non-negotiable to accomplish my goal:

Day 79____

Today's non-negotiable to accomplish my goal:

Day 80____

Today's non-negotiable to accomplish my goal:

Day 81

Today's non-negotiable to accomplish my goal:

Day 82

Today's non-negotiable to accomplish my goal:

Day 83____

Today's non-negotiable to accomplish my goal:

Day 84____

Today's non-negotiable to accomplish my goal:

Day 85

Today's non-negotiable to accomplish my goal:

Day 86

Today's non-negotiable to accomplish my goal:

Day 87____

Today's non-negotiable to accomplish my goal:

Day 88____

Today's non-negotiable to accomplish my goal:

Day 89

Today's non-negotiable to accomplish my goal:

Day 90

Today's non-negotiable to accomplish my goal:

90-DAY REFLECTION

Review the goal you set for the past three months. Did you reach your goal? Why or why not?

How did you grow as a person?

What challenges did you face with achieving your goal? How did you handle them?

What didn't go as planned? How can you improve on it?

Overall, how satisfied are you with the past three months, and why?

ABOUT THE AUTHOR

Elizabeth lives in Toronto with her two children and her dog. She has a B.A. in psychology and a master of education. With 20 years of teaching experience, Elizabeth offers both one-on-one and business coaching.

For more information, please email
elizabeth@thesmartcoach.ca

Visit www.thesmartcoach.ca

Follow Elizabeth on Instagram @thesmartcoach.ca

---

[i] Huberman, Andrew. "Toolkit for Sleep." Accessed July 5, 2023. https://hubermanlab.com/toolkit-for-sleep/

www.ingramcontent.com/pod-product-compliance
Lightning Source LLC
Chambersburg PA
CBHW061259140726
47998CB00006B/2281